Richard Rensberry

i

City Slicker's Guide to the Amish Country

Stories, Poems and Commerce from Fairview, Michigan

Richard Rensberry

ISBN-13:978-1-940736-18-1

Cover design by Richard Rensberry

Editors Mary Rensberry and Linda Halberton

Published by QuickTurtle Books LLC®

Published in the United States of America

DEDICATION

This book is dedicated to the free spirit, to the
Chippewa Indians and pioneers who forged a life
and living from Michigan's diverse and abundant
resources.
The name Michigan was apparently derived
from two Chippewa Indian words
meaning Great Lake.
The Chippewa tribe were hunters and gatherers
to the area before the settlements
of Mio, Fairview and Comins
came into existence.
The Au Sable River acquired its name
from the French that trapped and traded
along its banks.
It means— Sandy Bottom.
It is the heart of the Amish Country
and is our home.

Richard Rensberry

CONTENTS

Acknowledgements

I'd like to thank my lovely soul mate, Mary.
A special thanks to the residents
and business owners
from our local communities for their generous
contributions
in support of this project.
May the future be bountiful and prosperous for all!

Disclaimer

This book was conceived and written by **Richard Rensberry**. His views and opinions do not necessarily represent the views and opinions of any other person, their family members or acquaintances, charitable groups or business establishments, their associates or employees that are named or mentioned within the pages of this book. The views and opinions are those of the author, and the author's alone.

A Note to the Reader

This book does not purport to be a complete guide to the vast resources, activities and people that comprise the rural community that I have referred to as The Amish Country. It only scratches the surface of a magical land interacting and populated by the generous and hardworking souls of rural America. Here lies the commerce, stories and poetry of a morally and ethically sound group of diverse individuals that were too recently demonized by a presidential candidate as a "basket of deplorables". That short sighted and prejudiced mind-set is a product of an egotistically alienated academia and America's run amok agencies of mad-dog media and government.

City Slicker's Guide to the Amish Country is a guide into the heart and soul of a rural America still ruled by common sense, hard work, generosity and

God. You are welcomed with open arms into this rich and abundant landscape so unlike Washington DC, Detroit, San Francisco or New York City. Here, the old ways still abound in abundance, a blueprint to what many city dwellers now call the new ways—community support, organic foods, fresh air, free range beef, non GMO grains, chicken, pork, and lamb. It is a place dominated by peace, tranquility and self-reliance. This is a land insulated from ill-conceived regulations, TV propaganda, academia and intellectualism. Here resides down-to-earth hard-working, God-fearing doers and shakers.

Tread lightly and speak respectfully, open your eyes and look, open your ears and listen, there is much to be garnered and revered beyond the city limits of what you were taught in school. Life can be more than a career or a million dollar condo in New York City. It can be lived freely and undefined by institutional and governmental bureaucracy.

City Slicker's Guide
to the Amish Country

Richard Rensberry

Invitation

May your heart sing like the mockingbird, lilting
bright as the monarch in the marigolds, red
as the blood of the Indian paintbrush
flourishing at the orchard gate, happy
as the pears and the Sweet-Dutch apple, purple
as the sunburnt peach.

May your feet dance like the breeze
through the copses of oak and maple, waltz
like the rain through the roses and rhumba
up the walk to our back porch, shuffle
to the susurrus* of crickets and cicadas
'neath the stair where floorboards creak.

May the door open wide with a smile,
a hug and an ice cold drink.

*susurrus- whispering, murmuring or rustling sound.

The Lamp Maker

We live in a world in need of those with the magic of light. Men that can capture the glow and the twinkle from a witty man's eyes. Men with sight. Men with imagination and wands to cast spells of warmth and delight— a Merlin, Aladdin or Fairview's Lamp Maker.

Who? Mark Miles, the man who has made a quest to salvage the future from the past. The Amish Country's magician who can reach into a barrel and coax a genie into a bottle, a toaster or a Coleman lantern. He turns the ordinary into extra-ordinary lamplight. Lamps that chuckle, giggle or gossip from a living room table.

Mark Miles, a 20 year Navy veteran now spends time combing through the inventories of second hand stores and flea markets where he looks for objects that call out from our childhoods. Coleman lanterns electrified can give us everyday reminders of quality time spent with our dads and grandpas. Vintage kitchen appliances repurposed connect us visually to grandma's welcoming kitchen of years ago. You won't believe the variety of antiques that he transmutes* into lighting, end tables, rustic flag holders, chairs and wine glass holders; all with his unique Americana style.

You can view many of the Lampmaker's unusual designs on-line at his Facebook page: milesmakeovers, or for-sale in the windows of Fairview's favorite bargain store, the Sunrise Thrift Shop, a few hundred paces east of the traffic light at the corner of M33 and M72.

*transmutes- alters or changes into something different than its original purpose.

Squirrels

Squirrels are cute and amusing animals. Any football player would love the ability demonstrated by a squirrel's jukes* and fleetness of foot. Seeing them play in the yard and amongst the limbs of our birches and fruit trees brings a smile to our faces. They are great company and fanfare until that moment when their squirrelishness* inadvertently finds its way into your home. There they are rodents and their cute little smiles are transformed into devilish leers with razor sharp teeth. They chew on anything and everything because that is their inherent purpose and expertise in the eyes of The Lord.

I am not Elmer Fudd but I do draw the line where nature ends and civilization begins. Wild animals are meant to be in the wild, not incorporated into our society of family and friends, so it's vamoose or else for the wily little fellas.

My first attempt at eradication was polite conversation while sitting in my gliding chair on the back porch. They went so far as to sit there reverently chewing and listening before suddenly squirreling around in a game of wall clamoring tag. This little game was immediately followed by a burst of chatter and name calling. I can't exactly speak or understand squirrel but I am pretty sure there was a flurry of four letter words flung in my direction.

Amidst all this ruckus* I noticed a cute little redhead scamper and jump into the crawl space beneath our house and magically disappear through a hole the size of a fifty cent piece. Houdini would have been amazed and jealous.

As darkness descended I heard them joking and gnawing in bliss beneath the floor. I could hear their scratching and chewing escalating as the night progressed. At 3:00 A.M. they really started to party down. I, myself, cracked a beer and began plotting my retaliation maneuvers for when the sun would come peeking over the horizon.

When I was a teenager I had no qualms* about
shooting them with my pellet gun. Back then, it
somehow seemed like a viable and ethical solution to
my father's problems in the garden. My dad was rid
of a pesky varmint and I got paid bounty for every
squirrel tail I laid proudly on the granary floor.
Those tails kept me adequately supplied in root
beer and bubble gum. Unfortunately, my dad has
long passed and I no longer drink root beer or chew
Double Bubble*.

The Do-It Best hardware store would surely have
the answer to my dilemma sitting somewhere on their
well-stocked shelves and I found myself resolute
and determined to find it. I was sitting and waiting
patiently in the parking lot when the doors opened.

Poison was suggested as a good solution.

I mulled it over as I wandered down the aisles. In
the end, I decided on peanut butter set in a trap and
returned home.

I put a dollop on a small paper plate and set it out as trap bait. I had no choice, after all my home was under siege.

I figured it wouldn't take long before one of the boys came sniffing around. And sure enough, as I sat comfortably gliding in my glider on the back porch, a frazzle tailed little bopper came bopping across the yard and jumped unsuspectingly into my crawl space well.

I smiled. No squirrel can resist peanut butter.

Snap! Clang! Shuffle, shuffle.

I had him!

There had been no malice in my thoughts regarding the little redhead and her cortege* of squabbling boyfriends; that way of thinking was no longer a part of my adult makeup. To hurt them seemed unnecessary and unjust. The little boppers were harmless to the place they were headed- government housing on federal land down by the Au

Sable where they could frolic in the trees and squirrel around to their heart's content.

It would be hard to see the cute little redhead go, kind of like breaking up with the girl next door, but every man knows and comes to grips with having to end an ill-fated relationship.

I pray they find their rodent happiness in the house of The Lord instead of mine.

*jukes- quick, evasive moves.
*squirrelishness- a made up term meaning acting like a squirrel.
*vamoose- go away or depart hurriedly.
*ruckus- noisy uproar or disturbance.
*qualms- uneasiness or doubts, faintness.
*Double Bubble- bubble gum that came with a baseball cards inside.
*cortege- a number of followers.

Do-It-Best Hardware In Downtown Fairview

When it comes to a modern hardware store, Paul Ressler did it best. In 1994 the old feed store was remodeled to fit the modern "Do-It-Center" facade he had built in 1980. Paul had been at the reins since 1976 when Fairview Hardware and Lumber Inc. was split off from the lumber division of Boton Industries. Back then the hardware was housed in half of the building now known solely as the Fairview Food Market.

This, however, is not a lesson in history, this is a lesson in hard work, perseverance and family. When I sat down with Paul one of the first things that jumped out at me was a quote on the Hardware's Break Room bulletin board that reads: "In times of drastic change, it is the learners who inherit the future. The learned find themselves equipped to live in a world that no longer exists." Eric Hoffer, Prolific Author.

Philosophy meets reality at the Do-It-Best Hardware on the corner of Miller and Abbe Road.

Paul's learnedness has not only given the community "Do-It-Best" as a handy hardware store, but also as a philosophy for success. A tear welled up in Paul's eye when we talked about the store's future. "I am so blessed," he said, "to have Marika."

Marika is Paul's adept and learned daughter who is set to inherit the future— a sparkling next generation for the new and old Fairview Hardware and Lumber.

I am happy to say, Do-It-Best is here to stay!

Waltz of the Swallows

They came in
the heat of the day
to waltz
beneath the eaves
and awnings
in ritual waves
of figure eights,
swings and dips
of kamikaze wings
aflutter
in a game
of tag, touch
and kiss me
until maybe
just maybe
I'll be
your mate.

Purple Haze

Lilacs perform
the purple haze of spring,
explode like Hendrix*
full blast from the garden stage.
Honey bees sing
laden with gold.

*Hendrix- Jimmy Hendrix the guitarist.

Piano Instructor Jade Kozlow

Jade's unique path in life began at seven years of age when she discovered she had an aptitude and passion for music, especially the piano. Home schooled in Mio by her mother, Jade grew up with many unconventional opportunities not accessible to most of those schooled in a public institution. She was able to travel and nurture her musical passions far beyond the conventional classroom. She is now a certified piano pedagogy* as well as an early childhood music and movement facilitator.

Jade's expertise lies in teaching the piano and developing creativity and expression in toddlers through music and movement. She designs and implements her lesson plans to accommodate small classes of six or seven children aged infant to four. Her work is designed to help awaken and develop a child's innate abilities to internalize and feel diverse selections of rhythms and beats. Her classes are held at the Mio Baptist Church and the Skyline Event Center in Comins.

"It is amazing what infants and toddlers are able to learn," Jade shared, "when they are exposed to all the different meters and beats of music at an early age. Each individual child is allowed their own developmental pace both musically and physically. I am there in conjunction with their parents to guide and help that growth."

Jade emphasized that the early childhood movement work is done with a parent present and actively participating along with their child. She does not "babysit" or act as a substitute for daycare. Each lesson is structured and goal oriented and is delivered over a series of four to six class periods.

Jade graduated from Marnantha Baptist University with a degree in piano pedagogy. I found her to be highly communicative and engaging along with her great affinity for children and music. She is a joy and asset to the Amish Country arts.

*Piano Pedagogy- a method and practice of teaching musical skills to individual piano students.

High Speed

June has bloomed
and the roads are clear
of snow and human
stupidity. A trip to the city
of Alpena
for high speed Internet
from Cabin Creek Coffee and tea.

It's fifty three miles
one way
in my beat up truck
with wipers slapping in the hammering rain
that has come in answer
to feverish prayers for Amish grain
and the hungry brookies*
of McGinn Creek.

The blustering wind
buffets and blows
fifty into forty miles
where I park my truck

for coffee much, much sooner
than my friend the Trooper
was willing to abide.

*brookies- brook trout.

Help Wanted

Getting out of bed in the morning with a craving for a fresh brewed Cafe Latte or a Cappuccino goes gravely unfulfilled in the Amish Country. McDonald's Family Restaurant just doesn't fit the proverbial bill.

Someone with a passion and entrepreneurial sense could establish a thriving coffee and tea business somewhere in Fairview or Mio— I should think, without much stress. Who can resist the aroma and taste of rich coffees and blended teas from around the world. I love that old coffee house ambiance of warmth and camaraderie in a community. A gathering place where stories can take root and grow into legends.

How about some shelves with a rich array of organic spices and delectable herbs? Scrumptious honey-butter set on the tables— created fresh from a cache of Applebee Farm's liquid gold honey? An accoutrement* of locally canned Amish Country marmalade or mouth-watering jam to accompany homemade bagels and huckleberry scones?

A coffee house pastry and spice shoppe! In Comins, Fairview or Mio— Please!

*accoutrement- accompaniments to something.

Becky's Kitchen, 1547 W. Cherry Creek Road, Mio.

On a summer weekend trip to the Amish Bulk Store on Kittle Road you will discover an outside table loaded with a variety of freshly baked goods from Becky's Kitchen.

Becky Byler was born to bake and satiate your sweet tooth. She inherited a diverse rapport and knowledge of baking from spending her childhood under the tutelage of her parents in the family bakery. Now, with the help of her husband, Robert, in their newly opened bakery on Cherry Creek Road they produce a wide variety of health conscious breads, rolls, cakes, cookies, pies and fruit tarts.

What sets Becky's Kitchen apart are the ingredients. Their delectables are created from 100% fresh stone ground flours, coconut and olive oils, honey, maple syrup and non-GMO pure cane sugar. Her refreshing approach has been in part inspired through surveying their customers on what is needed and wanted for dessert.

When it comes to the fruit pies, they skip the fillers and gelatins and you get what you want, fruit! Simply yummy!

Their cookies, a local favorite, are soft and chewy.

The granola they produce is from gluten-free all natural oats and seeds.

With a summer visit to the Amish Country you can find their baked goods for sale at the Kittle Road Farmer's Market. You can also purchase their goodies from the table outside the Amish Bulk Store located at Kittle and Camp Ten Road. On a more personal basis, you can preorder directly from the Byler's countryside bakery at 1547 W. Cherry Creek Road and stop by to pick up your custom order fresh from the oven.

Roadside

The milkweeds tower
like castles from ditch's—
majestic displays
underneath silk leaves, parapets
of caterpillars, windows
and butterfly doors in iridescent
cocoons. Her blooms pose
between hive and bee,
a crown of jewels
for July to look
magnificent in purple.

Road Show

On the corner
of Weaver
and Cherry Hill Roads
Mary and I
spot a woodcock*
drunk as a duck
walking
the gravel
shoulder of road
where quack grass grows
three feet tall. We halt
the Honda
to gawk, chuckle and laugh
as four chesty chicks
wobble wobble
out of the ditch
one after another in tow
with their beaks like pipers
doodling a tune
in a sister and brother show.

*woodcock- long-beaked migratory bird. Upland
doodler.

Timberland Quilt Trail

Award winning quilter, Susan Shantz, conceived and created the Oscoda County Timberland Quilt Trail in 2012. Her artistic marriage between the area's old quilt heritage and her lively new designs can be found adorning 28 farms, charitable organizations, residences and businesses throughout Oscoda County. Each individual quilt is designed, laid out and hand painted on an 8' by 8' or 4' by 4' sign board block. Then, if you are friendly and blessed, you get it hung with the help from a local road commission volunteer and his lift-truck.

The quilt trail movement can thank Adams County Ohio for starting the first quilt trail craze back in 2001. There is now at least one quilt trail in every state of the union except Alaska and Hawaii, comprised of over 5,000 quilt blocks. The remarkable growth of this grass roots movement would be the envy of any newly formed advertising agency. In Michigan alone there are 26 different County quilt trails that are extant.

The base for the Oscoda County Timberland Quilt Trail is located at the Skyline Event Center just south of Comins across from the Woodworkers Shoppe. Those residing or doing business in Oscoda County that have interest in obtaining an individually designed quilt block for hanging on their business, farm or residence should contact Susan Shantz at 989-848-5757 for a consultation. Being part of the Timberland Quilt Trail is an excellent opportunity for boosting your business visibility and name recognition. Getting a quilt block designed, painted and put in place is by far one of the least expensive advertising opportunities I can recommend. QuickTurtle Books® has just put in its order for quilt block number twenty-nine.

Among the Amish

The Internet
has a hole in it
big enough for you
to slip into Fairview.
Our screens are black
except for the spinning
sunlit icon
that whirls and twirls
in some far flung google
gigabyte* galaxy.

Our Facebook
has gone faceless, our mouses
and spiders are blind, the phones
never ring and TV's an all purpose
blackboard of Post-Its
scotch taped with snapshots
of the kids to report
their wonderful and important news.

*gigabyte- unit of computer storage.

Skyline Event Center

In 1996 Michigan Magazine, a PBS show hosted by Del Vaughn and Barry Stutesman wanted to feature local businesses— Comins Lumber and The Woodworkers Shoppe on its TV show. Simon and Krystal Yoder, owners of Comins Lumber and The Woodworkers Shoppe collaborated with Michigan Magazine to build a log museum meant to showcase the many items donated by the various businesses featured on the TV show. The log building was then designed and built by Reuel Detweiler and donated to Michigan Magazine. It opened its doors to the public in 1998.

That aesthetically striking building as it stands today is known as The Skyline Event Center. It is located directly across the highway from The WoodWorkers Shoppe on M33 just South of Comins.

Michigan Magazine Museum ceased to function in 2012 and the building and grounds were leased to the Timberland Alliance of Oscoda County. Skyline Event Center carries on the mission and vision of Michigan Magazine Museum to promote Michigan entrepreneurship, arts and music. The Timberland Alliance's mission is to assist existing businesses in managing the growth of Oscoda County and fostering and attracting entrepreneurial minded individuals in a manner that strengthens the local economy while maintaining the rural character of the Amish Country Community. The Timberland Alliance serves as the driving force to promote the economic success and improve the quality of life for the businesses, residents, and visitors of Oscoda County and surrounding communities.

The Center graciously provides free high-speed Internet access to small businesses and individuals in the community. They are also proponents and promoters of local artists and groups. The Center can be rented for events large and small.

Amish Country Natural Products

Roxanne's Amish
delectables
deliver from the heart
in the heat of summer
when her blissful breads
rise hearty and fresh
from her bakery oven.

The warmth of her smile
spreads like butter
on her best rye toast. Her laughter
melts like Monk's sweet honey
on sour dough crust. Her pastries waft
all the way from Mio
to Comins, Luzerne*and Nirvana*.

*Mio, Comin's, Luzerne- local villages.
* Nirvana- a state of serenity achieved by the
enlightened.

Master Chef Josh Toensfeldt

Amish Country Natural Products begins with wholesome natural ingredients. The closer you get to the God given source, the closer you get to the real flavors, textures and nutrients served up by master soup chef, Josh Toensfeldt. Josh's command of spices and subtle flavors comes from years of experience creating his own homemade soup recipes.

Prior to gracing Mio with his culinary expertise, Josh prepared his delicious soups at High Noon Cafe in Jackson, Mississippi. He acquired a wide reputation for his tasty and wholesome soups made from seasonably fresh organic meats and fresh vegetables. Josh's move back to the Amish Country brought that organic and health conscious philosophy to the fresh soups he serves up at the Amish Country Natural Products store north of Mio. Some of his soups are Santa Fe Bean! Bean!,

Hoppin' John, Stone Soup, Tomato Rosso and White Bean Florentine to name a few.

Besides Josh's flavorful soups, The Amish Country Store has a variety of regional organic foods and local gifts. They have Pampered Beef, Sam Schmucker's free range chicken and an assortment of Heritage Farms free range pork. They also have fresh farm milk, cheeses and Roxanne's artisan breads baked right in store.

As a bonus, they carry a selection of QuickTurtle Children's Books written by my beautiful wife Mary and myself.

This Amish Country jewel is not to be missed by the health conscious or the gregarious of nature. Josh is full of friendly tales and culinary advice.

Oil On Canvas

Summer is born from the smell of turpentine and oils
on canvas.
It is a portrait of honeybees laden with pollen and
the hog-nose snakes
that masquerade the lane as cobras.
It is martins in the birdhouse and bats in the attic.

Summer is the lust that lives in the loam.
It speaks
of radishes, peppers, and yellow squash.
It seduces the onion
and brags about the taste of the lush tomato
that lives in the sun. The beets don't care. Their
blood is passionate
no matter the circumstance. And the peas, they
know the truth of openness
will always come. It is the corn that listens
to the depth the carrot and potato will go
to reach the cellar.

Summer is wading

the spring fed creeks, picking cowslips and violets to
set on the table.
It is making love in a bed of purple vetch
and building castles in the cumulus
clouds. It is long days
that lead to dusk when pheasants erupt from the
washes thick
with alder and pussy willow brush.
It is the ever presence of the hawk and crow, the
piles of stone
from which red sumac glows with a fire we capture
to light the barbecue.
We have friends and family
potlucks of beer
and bullshit.
We grill fresh perch and trout galore. We argue
and go to war
with mosquitoes.

Summer brings moths that come to the door
and beat their wings in Jesuit frenzy.
Crickets
conduct great symphonies to the firefly ballet
of lightning bugs
that flicker the lawn. The sky is full

of heat lightning. The moon
looks bigger than life.

Summer is like
that. It is a glutton of gifts from God to us
and from us to wives and family. It is art to be hung
on a friend's wall.
It is a wish come true. It is Happy Birthday.

Sweet Success Sugarbush

It is all about family and sugar maple trees when it comes to Abe Schmucker's organic maple syrup, cream and sugar. Tapping sugar maples for their sap has been a family tradition for many generations as spring comes to the Amish Country. The thaw-freeze cycles of March can seduce approximately 20 gallons of sap per tree into buckets for Schmucker's evaporator. It then gets boiled down into sweet liquid gold.

Abe's yearly production of 800 gallons of maple syrup is certified organic, meaning that it is uncontaminated by chemicals or cleaning agents. It is 100% pure maple syrup full of minerals and sweetness that is far healthier than conventionally processed syrups from the grocery store. The same applies to their beautiful dark amber maple sugar, it is sweet and healthy compared to such sugary alternatives made from corn syrup and processed cane sugar.

In the last weekend of March, Sweet Success Sugarbush hosts their annual open house for visitors to attend and experience the labor intensive making of maple products. During the event the Schmucker family also serve up samples of their sweet maple products along with chili, fresh bread and maple cotton candy. It's a fun filled occasion for young and old alike.

Their organic sugar and cream are sold locally at the Country Corner Bulk Food Store and their organic syrup is sold at Amish Country Natural Products. You can also stop by their farm located at 1442 N. Galbraith Road year around and purchase their products straight from the family. Just pull into the yard and ring the bell at Sweet Success Sugarbush.

Impressionism

I

Lightning strikes
a jack pine
near Abbe Road. Flames
lick at the split
severed trunk, leap
into a canopy
of tinder spruce
and dance toward self
created truth.

II

The pines survive
trunks charred.
The spruce stumps smolder
and smoke for days. The rains try
but fail to wash
the ash of holocaust away.

The dog days
of summer subside and relinquish
their feverish hold
and layers of frost and snow
lay bandages soft
upon ugly
scars of wounded times.

III

A patter of rain
helps spring thaw
into rivulets that gather
the gorge
Comins Creek. In the roar
small rodents
rustle and scamper to build
safe dens, deer
allay fears and fawn. The birds
return to their posts
to sing.

Vibrant
shoots of wintergreen, fern
and huckleberry emerge

with vigor and zest to paint
a magical landscape
surreal as Monet*.

*Monet- great impressionist painter.

The Family Bookshelf

What community can survive without a bookstore?

That is what Velma Esch asked herself and others in 1986. The Burning Bush across from the post office had closed its doors six years prior and no replacement bookstore existed anywhere in Oscoda County.

With the help of Paul Ressler (Do-It-Best-Hardware Owner), Reuel Detweiler, Carol Kauffman and others with a strong sense of community, faith and purpose, Family Bookshelf was born on the corner of Abbe and Miller Road. It now stands venerably and proudly where the old service station once dispensed gasoline instead of higher virtues and knowledge.

Family Bookshelf was founded as a non-profit bookstore and is staffed by many dedicated volunteers from the local community. A variety of books, cards, and gift items adorn its shelves. In the gift shop there is a leaning toward USA and

Michigan made products, and very dear to my heart, they carry an assortment of books authored by local writers such as Aaron K. Yoder, Joyce Yoder, Luman C. Slade, Vicki Kozlow, Ralph Moore, Mary DeMott, Norm Caldwell and yours truly, Richard and Mary Rensberry.

The Family Bookshelf also has an emphasis on Fair Trade items from third world countries such as baskets, book ends, musical instruments, jewelry, chocolate and coffee. They buy from Ten Thousand Villages, SERRV, Global Crafts, and Rafiki. The store recently added an Ohio based company that helps bring awareness to human trafficking, homelessness and addiction.

In 2017 Family Bookshelf will celebrate 30 years of serving the literary and religious needs of the little town of Fairview and the many outlying communities of Oscoda County. I recommend you stop by, buy a book or two and say hi to Linda, Leta, Lisa and the volunteers of which we are blessed. You may even catch me doing a reading from the pages of this book.

An Animal's Presence

Paradise dawns
for a doe and her fawns
in the wild flower meadows
and tall grasses
beside the music of Perry Creek.

Settled
in a suit of camouflage
and a fool's willingness
to photograph
mosquitoes, I wait.

A Kirkland Warbler
drops in. She hops
limb to limb
in a thorn berry tree
before her black eyes see
and flee my lens.

The soothing
susurrous of insects
and the deep green smell
of underbrush

yawns and pulls
my eyelids closed.

My feet go numb.
My head nods
until a puff adder hisses
and flicks its tongue
just a few feet away.

Camera ready
for an animal's presence
there's the squawk of jays
and chatter rants
from red squirrels that shatter
the hushed solitude
beneath the pine green canopy
where nothing moves
but a thought
that the jays and squirrels
have tattled on me.

The Magic Pocket

Breakfast at the Paddle Inn set the day up straight with bacon, eggs, hot coffee and a smiling waitress. It was a good place to unfold my county map and search out a place to enter a stream from a backroad. I was anxious for some brook trout fishing away from the hoopla of the Au Sable. The Au Sable is a great river for canoeing and kayaking but for fishing, it generally is as slow as watching snow melt in January. I leave fishing the Au Sable to the tourists if I am serious about catching my limit of trout.

Small stream fishing is not for everyone; it is a tough mosquito ridden journey into brush, chest high nettles and grass, poison ivy, ticks and a host of other hostile elements such as mud, invisible holes, snags, bees, ants and an occasional bear. Beyond those things it is like Alice In Wonderland, a wild world untamed by man and holding the miracle of catching brook trout as orange as the setting sun.

I laid my finger on Big Creek. There are acres and acres of Federal land giving access to this stream to the south of Luzerne, Michigan. It would take a lifetime to get intimate enough to really know her many curves. She wends and winds for miles on end.

Locating some consistently productive trout holes is a fisherman's quest that in the end will sew his lips tight, in other words, you will have to find them yourself. I have seldom divulged exact locations of where I regularly catch twelve and thirteen inch trout, for when I have betrayed that trust, those fish have found their way into the frying pans of those to whom I shouldn't have spoken.

Being this was basically a scouting trip, I had little expectation for what I might or might not catch. I just wanted to get my line in the water. Scouting is always a process of elimination with note taking that is either written down in a mental or paper journal. I have a very acute memory so my recording is all done in my cranium. (Pray I don't go senile or as the old saying goes, I'll be up shit creek.) The things noted refer to certain sections of stream: too brushy or access fairly easy, too shallow or some deep water, straight with no holes or wending with deep holes, what side of the stream gives the best access to the holes, all things that would either get me back or keep me from ever setting foot in that part of heaven or hell again.

From where I parked the truck, Big Creek looked promising right there at the road as it disappeared into a tangle of alders and tall grasses. It was brushy but not too brushy, the water looked to have a nice flow with some depth that looked promising.

I travel light with a telescoping pole that is over 40 years old matched with a cheap reel that can take some abuse. I have a canvas creel with my hooks, extra line, bait and a bottle of water. The collapsable pole is a huge advantage in navigating through the woods. It doesn't get caught in limbs or break during frustrating entanglements with blackberry bushes or dense thickets.

Since the water was looking promising right at the road, I settled down in some tall grass a couple of yards from the stream and readied my rod with a small swivel, some leader line and a number eight hook. I baited it with a medium crawler and flicked it delicately into the moving water where the current grabbed it and sent it swirling under the cut bank. I fed out a few feet of line and the crawler was aggressively snatched by a fish that had been waiting patiently for me to arrive.

Some fisherman's days are blessed with not having to grunt and grind our way through mud holes or stinging nettles. We don't have to go to war with mosquitoes and gnats, or dislodge broken sticks from our hair or our ears, we can just stand in the open in one spot and put a limit of nice brookies into the maw of our creel. Hallelujah!

The first fish I hooked and landed was a beauty, almost thirteen inches, then came a tidy eight incher*, then two identical twins of about ten. The last one was a bit more testy of my patience with numerable dry casts, but finally after some persistence I felt that welcoming tug as a fish sucked the crawler into its mouth and darted back under the bank. I waited a few seconds until I felt him again and set the hook. I was overjoyed by an aerial dance not that common from a brookie* before creeling* a beautiful full colored fish coming in at twelve inches.

I stood there and pondered my luck. The air was still cool and the sun had barely opened its eye over the horizon and I had my limit of brook trout for a nice lunch on the back porch. All I had to do was climb up the ditch embankment to my truck, no slogging through the brush for an hour or so from deep in the woods.

My mind noted and marked the spot as magic, and it will always remain so, even if I never happen to pull another trout from that little pocket of water ever again.

*incher- the length of the trout in inches.
*brookie- a brook trout.
*creeling- put a trout in a creel.

The Elk Country Gobblers

The Fairview area has won the distinction of being the wild turkey capital of Michigan. It has a huge population of healthy wild birds under the management of the Elk Country Gobblers. This local chapter of the National Wild Turkey Federation is headed by Frank Darling and has sixty-one local members that help to create and maintain a diverse habitat for these Thanksgiving Pilgrims to thrive. As a direct contrast to the mis-founded philosophy of the PETA organization and its disillusioned followers, hunters play an integral and important role in the successful wildlife management process. Without hunters the ability to create and maintain a healthy population of wild turkeys and other game in Michigan would fail.

A major portion of monies generated through hunting license receipts is used to fund such projects as the planting of native grasses, grains, berries, fruit, and crab-apple trees. DNR matched funds on a seventeen to one ratio are also used to purchase non-GMO seeds such as corn, soybeans, oats, sunflower and other wildfire seed mixes. These highly nutritional seeds are acquired locally from the Amish Country's Country Feed Supply in Mio. Habitat projects and supplemental winter feedings are then carried out through the volunteer efforts of the Turkey Federation's Members. Examples of these habitat and feeding projects recently completed can be found located on State Lands off Boiling Springs Road in Comins.

Large flocks of turkeys can often be viewed by taking a drive through the scenic countryside of the Amish Country. It is a diverse landscape of fields, hardwoods, pines, ridges and swamplands that provide a beautiful backdrop to these majestic birds.

If you would like to become a Federation member, a volunteer or just enjoy a family day of festivities, the Elk Country Gobblers hosts their annual Turkey Banquet the 3rd week of April. Their other annual events include a summer picnic and a family fun day at the Clinton Township Park in Comins. Please contact Frank Darling for membership details and family festivities throughout the year. He can be reached at: sparkncook@yahoo.com.

The Night Shift

The dreams come…
tossing and toiling
chainsaws that whine
through cedar and pine…
cord upon cord
to cut, stack and store…
wheelbarrows to roll…
stone to be picked…
tractors to start…
harrows to hone…
hay to be raked
and seed to be sown

when four forty-five
the dove's coo mourns
over fields still stubbled
with last years corn.

The Ire of God

Earl's heart
like the rabbits and deer
gets its tides from the phases
of moon. As it wanes
all is quiet in the woods
and furrows.

Out in the shed
behind double doors
you can hear Earl tinker
with his tools. By evening
he has staked his beans
and sweet green peas
to tendril their reach
for the sun.

At the onset of dusk
all the birds come
to make music
and the moon glows white
in the darkening blue
June sky. Fireflies
make twinkle in the yard.

We sit with our ears
tuned to the pipits
and warblers trill
in the white pine distance.
A wobbly-kneed fawn
bleats from the grass in the meadow
alerting a doe
that explodes from the thicket
with the ire of God.

Behind Earl's property
crooning howls
from a pack of coyotes
have a cadence of misery. Earl's rifle
reports the news
they shouldn't have come to intrude.

Pampered Beef

Tom Trimmer looks out
across acres and acres
of pasture on loan
from God. He knows
the farm like the Earth will spin
long, long after
he's gone,
that his hands are guests
like the beef he owns.

They all have names
like Larry, Curly and Moe,
Bugs Bunny and Big Dog.
Some are gentle
while others act mean
but all are pampered
free range and stress free
for lunch or supper
on local tables.

Crouched
on haunches

the carnivore prowls
like a beast in our genes, drooling
and whining
for a fresh steak
or a hamburger grilled
medium rare
somewhere in Mio, Lewiston
or Comins cuisines.

Tom Trimmer's Free Range Beef

Being omnivores, most of us enjoy a good burger or juicy steak. Yup, we like our beef! I like it happy both on and off the hoof. I like to see it frolic in the meadow as it fattens on grasses tempered by grains devoid of hormones and GMOs.

Please God! Let me witness such benevolent care bestowed by a rancher who knows how it feels at both ends of the food chain. Show me a herd full of joy!

"Tom Trimmer's Pampered Beef!" God says, is the answer to your prayers.

"Pampered Beef is free range, grass fed and content. It is without stress, hormones or GMOs. You'll find value here, far beyond the cost in dollar bills. It is delivered in taste, health and karma for all."

Tom's grandfather, Dr. Cecil Trimmer, a soft spoken veterinarian from Fenton Michigan, had a special gift with animals that he nurtured and passed along to young Tom. The legacy of that gift is now found in "Pampered Beef".

You can purchase Trimmer's pampered beef on and off the hoof by visiting Tom at his farm on Weaver Road in Comins, Michigan or you can pick up some freezer sealed pampered beef from the Amish Country Store between Fairview and Mio. If dining out is your pleasure, then Carrie James Restaurant in Comins has a menu of pampered burgers galore or you can enjoy a delicious steak at the Au Sable River Restaurant near the damn in Mio.

The Bear

Troyer saw the bear
in his field, the second
bear he'd seen
in his eighty-four years.
Our neighbors
down Dana Road
didn't see the bear
in their yard, but found
their feed barrel ransacked
in the night. The guy
on the hunting land
behind their trailer
saw the bear
stand up on its hind legs
and take a look
through the window
of their truck.

I saw the bear
last night while out
picking night crawlers
behind the shed

where I store equipment
and my stash
of brews. In the beam
of my flashlight
he looked harmless and scared
with jet black hair,
he looked vulnerable, naked
and overweight
with a bottle of beer
in one hand
and a fifth of whiskey
in the other.

Lawn Care

You won't find neon
flashing bright
to advertise Albert's
graveyard of parts,
just rumor, shelves and benches
piled with gears and lawn
trimmer blades, blowers,
mowers and tractors gutted
and stripped to the bone
like fish.

Some guy I met
at the barn sale said
Albert's is blind
but the man exists
and rubbed his chin
trying to remember
whether it was right or left
down Kittle Road.

I found it
up a long hill drive

beside a big white house
with bed clothes billowing
north to south
and a man flat
on his elderly back
with red hands raised
like berries dipped
in chocolate.

I asked and he was
Albert. My mower, I pleaded
was old, feeble and very sick
of lawn care; could he fix it
perchance, I wasn't in a rush
mind you, but my wife
and the quack grass were.

The Pioneer General Store

The Pioneer General Store became rooted in the Amish Country in the mid-eighties when Crist Hilty began a small mail order business that sold fishing gear, shoes and boots. Over the expanse of a few years Crist expanded the mail-order business into a store-front that included bulk foods prior to selling the business to Albert Miller in 1995.

The name pioneer and "entrepreneur" became synonymous and exemplified by Albert when he took over the reins of the business from Mr. Hilty. The original grass roots inventory was vastly expanded by Albert and divested off into two other stores: The Country Corners Bulk Food Store on Kittle Road and Shady Lane Footwear on Bills Road. Albert by then had conceived and given birth to the existing Pioneer General Store located on Mt. Tom Road north of Mio near Kittle Road.

The Pioneer General Store as it currently sits is now owned and operated by Albert's son Norm

Miller and Grandson, Norm Miller, Jr. It has become a blessing of all things useful for the community. Where else can you find time tested advice while Norm gives you a fill up of propane? How about a scythe for making quick work of that backyard burdock and thistle? Or maybe a tin of hard to find Bear Grease for your boots? Or my personal favorite, a popcorn popper that'll perfectly pop that tender white popcorn acquired from the shelves of The Bulk Food Store? There's something for everyone and every season of the year at the Pioneer General Store. It is a true to life general store with close-outs and a menagerie of old time and hard to find items you'll never acquire from a place like Walmart.

Being big on family, the Miller's Pioneer General Store also has a dedicated children's section with well-constructed toys meant to inspire a child's creativity for many years to come. The Miller children love to spend a portion of their free time at the General Store helping the family with the everyday tasks of the brisk business.

Of course, when spring thaws from a long winter and once again graces the Amish Country with an abundance of fresh vegetables, fruits and berries, you'll find all of the quality products you'll need and want for preserving next winter's stores.

Right from the outset the Millers have built and continue to maintain their strong motto that states — OUR BUSINESS COMPASS IS INTEGRITY, FAIRNESS, AND DEDICATED SERVICE for long-lasting relationships in the Amish community and beyond.

Tiny Tornadoes

The gnats have hatched
a morning cloud
of busy and dizzy
black tornadoes

as a flank of cowbirds
descend from the north
section of yard
like a special forces
planned assault

robins
move in from the south
while squadrons of swallows
swoop and dive
with reinforcements
from a pair of crows.

I get dressed
in old fatigues, grab my shovel
and smear my face
for all out war.

Exchange With Life

My neighbor does not get out of bed at five o'clock in the morning to don a shirt and tie. He gets up and gets dressed in a lawn mower or a snowplow. His command of machine and the environment is as if each were an extension of his own thought and appendages.

All you have to do is observe him at work and determine from the look on hi face that he loves what he does. He eyes each lawn and driveway like a sculptor would eye a virgin block of wood. Then he delves in with his tools. Zip, clip, zip. Vroom, vroom. He carves straight lines and sharp edges, all done with flare, presentation and conservation of motion. It's Zen* with blades and a weed whacker.

Creating is like that— it is a goal without ulterior motives, it has no nickels or dimes on the mind, it is not derived from drudgery or a need of compliments other than one's own.

Most people innately know that if they do it right, so will others. That is art. That is what it's like to be in exchange with life. You get paid in the end for what it's worth.

*Zen- seeking truth through introspection and intuition rather than from rites or scripture.

That Shantz Dang Ford

Old Gramps Shantz
had set the record
in the Antique Engine
and Tractor Show. Buffs
from towns around
were clamoring to see
and gossiping to know
the Shantz* dang Ford's
gear down ratio.

Whoa! Don't stall that FarmAll!
Don't use that clutch!
Don't brake that Deere!
Cuz them's the rules
or you're outta here.
For numb dumb slow, it's
finesse that throttle to putt putt low—
putt, putt sputter
putt, putt choke—

disgrace and shame
in a puff of smoke.

*Shantz- the owner of a Ford tractor.

Outside the Box Arts

When Susan Shantz was a child, she was awed by the beautiful quilts her great grandmother, grandmother and mother were able to create with their hands. Though may years passed before Susan eventually discovered that quilt-making was a passion that had threads to her soul, she has since made quilting a way of life. As founder and owner of Outside the Box Arts, Susan designs and creates quilts that are both modern and steeped in her ancestral traditions.

Her quilts are a mastery of complex design and bright colors that come to life with a vibrancy and warmth to enhance any room's decor. To spin her quilting magic, Susan works freehand and free motion on a longarm A1 Elite 923 machine.

As creator of the Oscoda County Timberland Quilt Trail, Susan's quilt designs also transcend the medium of needle and thread and are transformed into quilt blocks for local barns and businesses throughout the Amish Country.

To view Susan's work you can visit her on Facebook and Instagram at OTB-ARTS. She offers a variety of quilting services, including quilt design: from simple to complex, binding, sleeve hanging, back seaming and squaring, etc. She is eager to work with both novice and pro to get the quilt pattern and services you are looking for. She can be reached at: 989-848-5757.

Fairview Volunteers

We have had a crop of volunteer tomatoes pop up every spring since I planted a couple of organic plants a few years ago. These tomatoes are an extremely determined bunch. They produce large healthy crops of golf ball size tomatoes that are juicy and delicious. Last year we decided to throw a half dozen ripe tomatoes into pots containing dry dirt. We left them in dry pots all winter and in the spring we added water to the pots. Hundreds of young tomato plants burst from the soil in just a few days. After some painstaking thinning we had a couple dozen healthy young plants growing in the garden.

As the plants matured I tried to train them with wire tomato cages but lost the battle. These plants grow like poison ivy. They love to spread out over the ground sending tendrils off in all directions, voracious as weeds. They just produce and produce. Last year we had tomatoes until the frost finally got to them. I just never recorded the breed, so I'll call them the Fairview Volunteers and stash away a bag of seeds for safe keeping.

These Fairview Volunteers grow in large cherry tomato-like clusters, but tend to be a bit larger in size. We get several pounds per picking, filling a medium size grocery bag. I did not think to record the date the plants emerged from seed, but a good estimate is that we had ripe tomatoes in about 70 days. Teamed with fresh lemon limes, peppers and cilantro, my wife Mary canned enough pints of salsa for two jars per week for six months. That's a lot of hot sauce. Better yet, we are still eating the fruit and making lots of fresh organic tomato soup, cucumber and tomato salads and BLTs. I expect to have these tasty treats until the frost once again steals them away for another winter of enjoying Mary's hot and tasty salsa.

The Food Chain

Whitetails in the night
munch tomatoes, spinach
and corn, devour them all
with cilantro and sugar
peas, grind them
to a pulp with yellow
teeth and belch
artichoke mist
beneath brisk starlight.

The parsnip and beans
are stripteased and abandoned
stalk-naked.

Leaf after leaf
it's a lettuce feast
with cucumber
and zucchini squash, of pumpkin
and potato mash
as carrots are pawed
from the earth and crushed
with raspberry radish

puree, even the prickly
leaves of blackberry
get no mercy.

On our menu today:
it's habanero, jalapeño and venison
steak.

The Reaper Carrie James

Somewhere in the upstairs
the Reaper creeps
with heebie-jeebie* friends
that hackle hairs on the back
of your neck. They play tricks
dimming lights
as the floorboards creak.

With all rumor aside
Carrie James up and died
from nothing more devious
than age; no grudge to stage
on the souls death left behind.

Maybe she's a hoax
or maybe she's a spook
who just likes to cook
on a Friday when locals
need spice. Be sure

when you dine
to set your phones
and your spine
to ghost-mode vibrate—
because maybe you might
just maybe you might
get a call from The Reaper
Carrie James.

*heebie-jeebie- poetic license adjective meaning
spooky.

Fairview Flooring & Mattresses Direct

Why would anyone in this "got to have it right now" world, make a phone call to schedule an appointment with Peter Szubelak about buying carpeting or a mattress? Then drive a mile off the beaten path to meet him at a warehouse?

Are people that curious? Maybe, but I would bet it's because people love to save money, and lots of it?

Peter's innovative business acumen* of bare bones overhead and lack of storefront labor costs allows him to pass generous savings onto the customer. Sometimes savings of as much as 25 to 50 per cent under retail.

Instead of wasting away in a sales room, Peter is out and about in the community helping and steering his customers into making better informed decisions regarding product and value. He tries to offer a more expensive and higher quality product at a medium level price. That is an enormous asset because the results of cheaply made products are a dire lack of longevity and that in the long run equals more expensive. If you want to buy and install cheap products you can find all of those you ultimately can't afford at a Walmart or Home Depot. Fairview Flooring & Mattress Direct does not waste time, effort and your money on something that has little or no value over time.

Peter has spent the last eighteen years in the flooring business for the purpose of making an honest to God living not a pie in the sky killing. He simply strives to deliver good products at a good value. No hoopla, no pitches, just down to earth common sense and sound business practices. That is specifically why my wife and I chose to have our carpets replaced and installed by Fairview Flooring during our recent move to the Amish Country. Good product, good value. We are now shopping for a softer mattress and plan to take Peter up on his invitation to come on down for a softer than firm test nap. Ah!!!

To make an appointment, you can reach Peter at: 989-848-8700 for all of your flooring and sleeping needs.

Bulldozer

The paths in the sumac
were all known by heart,
the strawberries and pin-cherries
were wild and tart,
it was here my gifts
for mom did grow,
the black-eyed Susan
and the pussy willow.

There were zebra worms*
with horns on their heads,
and lady slippers
in their wintergreen beds,
and high on a limb
in the old beech tree,
we had a house
my brothers and me.

But they hollered and cursed
and they dug and they dozed...
for them it was sweat, a ditch and a road.

*zebra worms- striped caterpillars.

Reality

I wanna dance
down the throat
of a humming spring,
I wanna float
like a note
from a guitar string,
I want to twirl
like a pearl
in the summer sun,
I wanna curl
in a tub
of sweet alyssum
but I got to paint the house.

Woodworkers Shoppe

Construction products in The Amish Country would be severely lacking if not for the Woodworkers Shoppe located on M-33 between Fairview and Comins. This one-stop-shop for log home products, managed by Gary Gee, carries such unique products as Barn wood Paneling, custom log kitchens, log stairways, and log mantles. These unique interior design items cannot be found anywhere else in the north country.

They also carry a wide selection of interior design products— such as knotty pine paneling, cabinetry, wood doors and flooring harvested and milled locally from the area's abundant forests. You will also find a variety of exterior log products— such as log siding, peeled logs, railings and stairs for your homegrown exterior needs.

Besides the construction products there is a vast selection of decorating items as well. Log and wood furniture hand-crafted on site at The Woodworkers Shoppe is readily available to enhance and give your home that comfortable, wood-crafted feel. You can even light your log creations with USA made rustic lighting fixtures that are exquisitely designed and meant to last. Of course, Gary's renowned photographs are there to give each and every room its final touches. You can peruse his photography gallery at: photographyupnorth.com.

The Woodworkers Shoppe is far from your run of the mill sawdust and glue joint. This is the real deal made from local timber logged and milled by Comins Lumber. It is where I purchased the raw materials for my own custom built mantle. Great stuff! Great care! Great service!

Even if you are not visiting Northeastern Michigan in person, you can still Shop-Their- Shoppe at their detailed informational website: woodworkers shoppe.com.

Purchases/shopping can also be made 24/7 online at: loghomeshoppe.com.

Fairview

Before Detroit
bared concrete teeth,
before asphalt
and creep of houses
raped the rivers
and crystal streams, before stacks
spewed blackened ash—
snow lay white across the land
and silence
was like the hand of God
had descended Heaven—
the print of man
was but a moccasin, progress
had not yet been measured
by Henry Ford.

A Day In the Country

Breakfast is cooked
and put on the table, the cows are milked
and hay in the stable, the chickens are fed,
butchered and bled when the sun comes up
to whip, whisk, wisp the sky rose red.

The tractor is gassed
and the mower blades honed, the hay laid flat
is raked and combed, lunch is served
in back of the truck, the mower unhitched
gets ditched for disc, harrow and dust.

Supper is baked
chicken and bread, fresh green lettuce
with horseradish spread, peppermint tea
from a pantry cache with ice cream churned
from butterful* lows of udder full cows.

The books are swept
for dollars and cents, the bills are paid
and laid to rest, the muscles are scrubbed
and the teeth are brushed- when down we lay

naked and hushed— for a batch of sweet
country hugs.

*butterful- contented sound.

The Steiner Museum

What if the past had a mind and a pair of hands?
What if it could reach out from its distant location in
history and drop a mill stone into present time. What
if you could hear it grinding whole wheat into flour?
Would you wish to catch a whiff and a glimpse of
stone-ground flour through the eyes and nose of
your past? I desired just that and carried my hopes
to the Steiner Museum just north of Fairview on M33
at Reber Road.

Though I didn't find that working millstone, I
found within its confines a vast history of artifacts
that embraced the lives of those that lived to put
whole and nutritious foods upon our tables. The
vibrations and sounds of those hardworking souls
still reverberate from the harvesting and processing
tools salvaged and on display throughout the
buildings and grounds of the museum.

You can wander an era before the pesticide
farming and Monsanto's reign, when men with hoes,
scythes and twine patiently worked the grain fields

and rows of corn. You can step into pioneers' clothes and shoes for a moment or two, imagine the sweat and dust as it collected on their brow. With a discerning eye at a well-worn hitch you might even garner the root meaning of the word horsepower.

This Memorial Day when the Steiner reopens for the season, you should see a prominently placed resurrection of the Royce millstone display somewhere on the museum's grounds. The millstone was in operation from 1890 until 1910 producing stone-ground wheat for area residents. You as well, should find a repaired and renovated Yerkers Finnan lumber planer that was once owned and operated locally in Mio by Domer Miller in the early nineteen hundreds. This cumbersome behemoth, though no longer a part of American production, has an awe inspiring mechanical beauty restored by Norm Caldwell, the Museum's caretaker.

The Steiner Museum should definitely be a part of everyone's itinerary for immersion into the lives of the settlers who first farmed and lumbered the Amish Country.

God's Bosom

Back in the arms
of Michigan.
I'm in love with you,
so beautiful.
Back in the arms
of Michigan
your heart speaks soft
and true.

Back in the arms
of Michigan.
Without you I would weep
so incomplete.
Back in the arms
of Michigan
cradled and rocked
to sleep.

Highland Lumber

If you are new or a grizzled veteran of the Amish Country and you are in the market for a custom built home, Highland Lumber of Mio is a one stop provider. They'll take you from architectural design and blueprints all the way through to your first step over the threshold into your dream house. Highland's Paul Yoder has personally slipped his feet into a well-worn pair of work shoes and remains the driving force behind mobilizing and employing many talented local contractors to do multi-faceted building. From generals* to subs*, these contractors and their crews manage and build custom homes, kitchens, baths, garages and pole barns conceived and designed through the helpful guidance of Highland Lumber's staff. Highland Lumber conveniently delivers and operates within a 125 mile radius of their Mio lumber yard located on Kittle Road.

For the do-it-yourselfer, Highland Lumber also provides all the raw building materials necessary for each phase of your construction project at a very competitive rate. Their large inventory of tools and supplies will enable your tool belt and tool shed with all the correct implements for the job. They are the one stop shop for the Amish Country building industry.

If you are a stickler on supporting local economies like I am, they also carry an assortment of Michigan produced doors, trim and paneling for both interior and exterior needs. They carry Michigan produced pallets and custom rough sawn lumber produced and milled by local millers. Their resume of custom homes is all inclusive from that small retiree's dream to that million dollar mansion.

This is a big countryside. If you would prefer not to spend a lot of time traversing it from one end to the other, I'd check out the many benefits of getting to know the staff and services offered at Highland Lumber. By visiting their one stop shop, may your home find a secure and permanent footing in the Amish Country!

*general- general contractor that manages and directs all phases of a construction project.
*sub- specialized contractor that does one phase of a large construction project such as plumbing, electrical, sheet rock, painting, etc.

Clean Hands

Oh, Great Spirit
whose voice I hear
in the winds,
and whose breath
gives life to all
the world, hear me:

I come before you,
one of your many
children. I am small
and weak. I need
your strength and wisdom.

Let me walk
in beauty,
and make my eyes
ever behold
the red and purple
sunset. Make my hands
respect the things
you have made. Make
my ears sharp to hear

your voice. Make me wise
so that I may know
the things you have taught
my people— the lesson
you have hidden in every leaf
and rock.

I seek strength
not to be superior
to my brothers, but
to be able to fight
my greatest enemy—
myself.

Make me ever
ready to come
to you,
with clean hands
and straight eyes,
so when life fades as a fading
sunset, my spirit may
come to you
without shame.

by Yellow Lark (Sioux Chief)

Rain Dance

Great Spirit
with your fertile patter
of feet, come! Come
in the clouds of my dreams! Kiss me
as you kiss Mother Earth, Great Spirit
with your fertile patter
of feet. Come! Wake!
with your drumbeat chants, cleanse
with your tom-tom dance! Shake
with your belly full of laughs! Great Spirit
with your fertile patter
of feet.

When War Comes

He was my Older Brother by spirit, not by blood.
He could look through the eyes of a crow or a hawk
and see a person even when they weren't present or
nearby. He had what the elders called "far vision".
He had the ears of a deer and the wings of a duck.
He could disappear at will.

I adored him.
He told me, "Stop being a puppy, Young Bird."

He often came to me decorated with paint in the
colors of a warrior. He pointed with a finger and
spoke with his hands. He would grab my tongue and
give a quick shake of his head if I spoke too loud
near the stream where we fished for trout. He gave
me feathers for lessons and beads rubbed raw by
the swirling currents of the Au Sable River. He
gifted me the paw of a weasel when I showed him a
nest of woodcock eggs.

I looked up to receive his praise.

He told me, "Don't put your eggs in another man's basket."

He helped me choose and cut an ash to make a bow. He taught me the way of sticks and how they fire-harden just right as they plead to be an arrow. He showed me rituals on how to con a feather and honor the flint when it is broken. I was coached on how to say the exact words to make an arrow fly true to its goal.

I found truth in what he said.

He told me, "Truth is worthless to those that are dead."

He tested me like the leather I had tanned to string my bow. He tested my patience and the edge of my will. He approved or disapproved. It just depended on the direction of the wind. I could tell by the lift of his chin when he knew that I knew.

I smiled at his knowledge.

He told me, "A lesson learned is a lesson you forgot."

We practiced until I bled and my blood became
the vessel that poured my spirit into arrow and bow;
until my hands were indistinguishable from the rose
of the wood. I shot arrow after arrow, day upon day
two years in a row. I could stand on my head or I
could sit, I could run or I could crawl. It didn't matter
to my arrows, they had learned to arrive where I had
meant them to go. They were I, I was them and in an
instant I could snatch an arrow out of flight and
whisk it back from where it came.

I was cocky with my aim.
He told me, "The pheasant that crows too soon
and too loud gets eaten."

He took me to the timber and taught me how to
hunt like the big cats, how to climb like a goat. I was
shown the camouflage of faces painted and the
different spirits they can conjure for the hunt. He
spoke the words behind the smoke and the rhythm
in the drums. We danced all the dances, chanted all
the chants and in the Spring I came to be a man in
the outstretched arms of Silver Birch.

I went to her often in the night.

He told me, "Love is a warrior's strength and his weakness combined."

We sat in silence amidst the bustle of the many young boys who ran in search for themselves and our arrows. They plucked the shafts from the grass where we practiced and brought them back to our quivers delivered by name. We traded for their efforts with feathers and stones or candy for those that shook their head. One That Grows Fat In the Middle is my brother by blood. My Little Brother in spirit is Cloud In the Eye. He too has taken a liking to candy above feathers and often cries at my words of dismay. I do not recall myself in his childish manners. He seems to lack the will in search for his honor.

Older Brother clicks his teeth. He points and gestures with his chin, "Some boys are men, some boys are squaws. It'd good to know which," he said, "when war comes."

The Oracle

On the corner
of Schmid and Oaks*
sits the all knowing
crow, conspicuous
in his finest
hat and black robes
glistening
purple and gold. He is
the eyes, ears
and mouth
of Fairview.

The whitetails twitch
in Troyer's field
and carefully listen, the gophers
sniff and surface
for a quick glance out the back
door. Even the bees
gone loopy drunk on lilac pause
for a snippet
of the latest news.

It's just a Mennonite's
tractor pitching gravel
up the road.

*Schmid and Oaks- country roads

Lets Talk Auction

When I go to an auction it is reminiscent of the carnival games I once enjoyed as a kid. Sometimes your bid ends up a winner, sometimes a loser. The thrill is in the game to buy something valuable for cheap, but it takes discipline to know when to buy or walk away.

LETS TALK AUCTION on the corner of M33 and Perry Creek Road in Mio has become my carnival. It's an all day affair jammed pack full of opportunities to acquire anything and everything one may or may not need. How about a 1957 Austin FX3 London Taxi Cab? Or an arsenal of guns and ammo that belonged to Norm Olsen before he hightailed it to Alaska? Maybe a Victorian baby coffin?

Donna Tuttle, an award winning auctioneer, dispenses of such goods like a coffee percolator percolating on double espressos. Greg Tuttle, who started in the auction business at the tender age of fourteen, controls the proceedings like a maestro conducting a symphony. All is done under their warehouse big top once owned and operated by Vern Gerber.

The Tuttles, being perfectionists, operate the family auction with a high regard for ethics and integrity. They once were commissioned to clean out and auction the contents from an old barn stuffed full of non inventoried goods and buried in amongst the junk they found a foot locker filled with old coins worth untold sums. Many would have simply loaded up the goods as their own, but that is not the way Greg and Donna do business. To them it would have meant a future of untold bad karma not to turn the coins over to the seller's estate. That is someone you want to do business with.

Lets Talk Auction has also hosted a variety of charity auctions for area schools and community groups. Donna has the distinction of being the first woman auctioneer to walk the talk at the annual Mennonite Relief Sale.

Every Thanksgiving Day, Lets Talk Auction has their annual Christmas auction from five o'clock to around midnight. People attend from far and wide to bid on a wide variety of brand new items, such as toys, tools, and sports equipment. This annual event has been held every Thanksgiving since 2003. The rest of the year auctions are held Saturday morning.

So if you are looking for great deals, great entertainment and great people, LETS TALK AUCTION is a wonderful show. Highly recommended.

Cities of the World

Dirt
has been slandered
and labeled a pile
of dirty names. It has gathered
to itself
human traits
for a bad reputation
and can't seem to clean
itself up, confess or repent. It means
too many things
to too many different people, like something
to be swept off of
or under the rug, something to wash
with advertising or scrape from beneath
a dead or a guilty man's
fingernails. Dirt
has become the prize so sought
by special interests
like vacuum cleaner salesmen,
by lawyers and politicians, by magazines
and newscasters
who love to smear and wallow
in the world's worst. It was

the not too distant past
when dirt meant dirt
like loam, clay, gravel or sand.
The kind and nature of it
meant all the difference
between living and dying
to the farmer and his worms, it meant
meat or no meat to set on the table,
vegetable or no vegetable
to put in your salad; oils, nuts
and fruits, wheat
for bread and corn for chips, it meant
essentials like salsa
and beer. Dirt

is still what it is
when hauled away,
when buried by concrete
or sequestered beneath
sidewalks and banks, it holds the future
and our cities of the world in place.

Triple "B" Heritage Farm

As I drove up the long drive off W. Cherry Creek Road, I was struck by the natural habitat on which I viewed huge and happy hogs freely roaming and grazing. These were beautiful animals full of joy and thanks. They eyed me with a smile.

I had first encountered Robert Byler and his wife Becky at the Farmers Market on Kittle Road. They were selling vegetables along with Becky's scrumptious baked delectables. It was there that I had vowed to seek Robert out to make him a part of this book. His aura of friendliness and enthusiasm are irresistible. It is that same spirit on which the hogs are nurtured and raised at Triple "B" Heritage Farm.

Robert has been in the business of pasture raised hogs for five years. He has a herd of over 100 hogs grazing 22 acres of seeded rye, oats and turnips. Besides the free range pork, Robert sells grass fed lamb, beef and chicken out of his farm yard freezer.

My wife Mary and I purchased two loin roasts, one for making tamales and the other to barbecue as we basked in the final days of Indian Summer. The tamales were delicate and delicious. The barbecued loin roasts were hands down the best pork I had had since I left my father's farm in the early 1970's. There is no substitute for care and respect when it comes to farming animals and Robert and his family do it right. No hormones or GMOs intrude here, just all natural and farm fresh.

Robert's pork is available for purchase at the Amish Country Store just off the big bend on M72 between Fairview and Mio. You can also visit his farm on N. Cherry Creek Road and view first hand what it means to be a farmer instead of a manager in a meat factory. Huge difference! Huge rewards in taste and healthy living.

The Mouths of Hollywood

It has come to utensils
like knives and forks,
the ax and the Smith and Wesson.
It is chicken, fillet mignon
and a rack of lamb. It is the Oscars
and the Grammys. It is what people eat
without blood on their hands.

Where do they teach them
this division of meats
from butcher to table. It is like
how you crap and it's gone
in a swirl down
the sewer out of sight.

Hollywood isn't real, you know.
It's a city of actors on a set, a place to forget
all the blood and tears.
The laughter is fake. None of them
get up in the morning
to the smell of death
and strop of a knife.

One Bullet

We the people
within reason
maintain our integrity
to defend

our freedom of religion,
ourselves, our families
and the Constitution
of the United States. We refuse

to bend
when it comes to criminals,
political correctness
and the Second Amendment.

We the people
within reason
believe our Nation
is under God, indivisible
with inalienable rights
and justice for all.

To the republican
and the democrat,
to the socialist, the liberalist
and supreme justices,
to the universities and psychiatrists
going weak in the knees
on common sense— until
we see higher purpose, true awakening
of judgement and reason
within self, nation and the world,
we will relinquish our guns
          one bullet at a time.

D&M Guns

Off the beat'n path in Lewiston sits the friendliest gun store in Northern Michigan: D&M Guns. It takes a little do'in to find it, but once you do, Denise and Mark Lesar are fully armed with an assortment of guns and accessaries to outfit both men and women. Not only are the prices some of the best around but you are rendered the personal touch that can be afforded only by proprietors. Their true to life motto is "COME IN AS A CUSTOMER, LEAVE AS A FRIEND".

Women in particular can expect the utmost care and tutelage under the knowledgeable presence of Denise. She can educate you on the best gun and accessories for a woman, be it a revolver or semi-automatic with a matching concealed carry purse and under gear. Even if you are a complete novice when it comes to guns, you can feel assured they will enlighten and help raise your comfort level.

D&M Guns is also a place you can just hang out and have a complimentary cup of coffee. You can shoot the breeze or seriously engage yourself in the process of owning a gun.

On one occasion a customer wandered in and asked if Mark could adjust his rifle scope. Denise noticed not one, but three bloody crescent moons adorning the fellows brow.

"Got scoped, did Ya?" she asked.

"I did. I thought I was just crowding the scope so I hung back and fired a second time," he replied with humor and fingered the second moon.

"Apparently that one didn't cure Ya, neither," Denise added, unable to suppress a chuckle.

"I do admit, I fired again." He fingered the third scar, "I am not the brightest light in the socket."

Everyone had a good natured laugh as Mark got out his tools and adjusted the ill placed scope.

The fellow returned to D&M Guns a month or so later with a big smile minus any new moons. True to their motto, he is now a regular customer and a friend.

So choose right and choose responsibly, choose D&M Guns for all your firearm and accessory needs. I did and their services were exemplary.

The Seeds of Socialism

When it comes to obstacles
some children run
to their mothers, others
stand up and spit
in the eye
of adversity.

Some children cry
at seeing their blood
and fear that which
spilled it, others
are surprised
but get immune to it.

Some children fit
their shoes to their feet,
while others will fit
their feet to their shoes
and grow bunions
and callouses instead of judgement.
Some children scream
to get their way, they fuss and run
to the government.

The Waiting Room

People sit
in a waiting room
unaware of the vampires
that hover
in the corner of the room in a box
just waiting
for some sucker to push the button
that turns them on.

Anderson Cooper
with his snarky little smile
and white cap
is sharpening his teeth
for Donald Trump, he speaks
of gayness as fitting
the life styles of everyone
in their chairs waiting
for something to cheer about.

In Florida
a sick man made sick
by a sick psychology has murdered

innocent people. This horror
isn't sad or bad enough for CNN's thirst
for blood, they want to suck
all hope and optimism
into the darkness of their black
box.

I myself, have harbored an arsenal
of silver bullets. I have
fortified my guns
with supplements of onion
and garlic. I stand
to brandish a stake, faith and a crucifix
in the face of CNN.

Chicken Little

When I was a kid, I would look searchingly up into the far reaches of blue sky. Every so often I'd spot a speck of spiraling danger. When I did, I'd dash into our farm house and grab my twenty-two rifle in defense of the vulnerable hens and chicks. As I crouched beneath an apricot tree, I would watch and wait patiently as the speck grew bigger and bigger until it became so imminent a dark shadow was cast across the yard. Then I'd take aim.

That is the way I feel today. I look out into Corporate America and see looming specks like Home Depot, Walmart and Monsanto. I envision their bean counters and hawkish executives sitting around conference tables sipping coffee and conspiring over their devious plots. These men are no different than the chicken hawks that lurked and circled above in my youth.

As an adult, I fear for our local businesses whose importance to the local community is bigger than New York. It is bigger than Donald Trump. It is bigger than the profits of Walmart and Home Depot combined. Local business is the epitome of what makes America great, it is the thread that sews the roots to the tree and the tree to the sky when it comes to integrity and care for every person that walks through the door of a locally owned business. These local businesses often stock and sell USA made products that Home Depot and Walmart have negotiated to import for a fraction of the cost; and dare say, I fear the speck grows bigger.

Just this year I watched as Dollar General sunk its talons into the local economy. It's only a few dollars China and the Wall Streeters pluck from our pockets. Nothing serious, nothing to get alarmed about. We can shamelessly walk in through their doors and the sky won't fall. When we exit, it is still just a tiny speck circling in the heavens overhead.

It is the future I worry about, sometime when a distant winter takes its grip and someone atop a high rise in New York conceives there is profit to be had in Mio. He sticks a push-pin into a tiny dot that marks the spot; a sticky note with details on all the different properties for-sale along the main road out of Mio toward Fairview.

In the spring, all of us wake to the revving of bulldozers. Everyone gawks in wonder and awe as the excavation and construction takes shape. In no time at all their grand opening signs line the highway. Walmart or Home Depot, it doesn't matter. Local businesses will hear the sinister screech of these birds. A customer here and a customer there will find their bottom lines less stressed by the bargains from China. The screech will become a feeding frenzy as Wall Street's corporate culture rips into the remains of small business in the Amish Country.

I say, nothing cheap is worth the price of a soul. God help us value and keep it so. Please shop home-grown businesses that support and nurture our local economies.

QuickTurtlesque

QuickTurtle Books® is like a three year old toddler, full of life and curiosity for the world into which it was born. Founded in 2013 as a publisher of children's books, QuickTurtle Books' first adventure and duty was to pick up an illuminating flashlight and shine its penetrating beam into the dark underworld of pharmaceutical giants and psychiatry. There it found two co-conspirators diligently at work labeling and drugging millions upon millions of healthy and defenseless children for obscene profits into the billions. Under the guise of such controversial mental and learning disorders as ADHD, these Gotham City villains were found to be perpetrating onto an unsuspecting public one of the biggest money making hoaxes in world history. The book's title when first published was called IT'S BLACK AND WHITE. The book's current designated title is QUICKTURTLES RULE and is a must for helping parents, teachers and children stand up and say no to these modern day charlatans and their forked tongues. Also on the

141

drugging and drug prevention front, Richard has authored a modern day fable called HOW THE SNAKE GOT ITS TAIL which tackles recreational marijuana proponents head-on.

On a lighter note, QuickTurtle Books® also publishes fun and uplifting books such as CHRISTMAS CHRISTMAS EVERYDAY and COLORS TALK. They have several more such books in the pipeline. They have a locally set children's book about the AuSable Railroad as well as GOBLIN'S GOOP, a story about a swarm of revolutionary bugs that do battle against an evil empire. Author Richard Rensberry also has two books of modern poetry, WOLF PACK MOON and THE LOVE TREE. All QuickTurtle books are for sale in local area bookstores and on Amazon.

Like all children, QuickTurtle Books® can't sit still, they squirm in their seats and can't play quietly. They love to get into mischief and poke sharp sticks into the proverbial bees nest. Their conformity is to the best welfare of the Reader, not to the politically correct norms of mainstream media. Buy and read locally grown QuickTurtle Books® and may you embrace being QuickTurtlesque.

Silence

Ribbons of perfect corn
roll over the hills and stretch for miles
devoid of milk, pig
and other weeds. Rivers of Roundup
Ready beans undulate
pest free in the summer breeze. Acres
of sunflowers
bow their heads, yellow faces
sad and in obedience
to Dupont and Monsanto; you can almost hear
their silent prayers
reach forever.

In the meadows
of long grasses, in the orchards
of red apple and down the roads
of hard gravel, between posts
strung with barbed wire, in the thistle towers
and along the infinite lines for electric power,
there is silence, a silence unbroken
by wren or sparrow,
by lark, finch or whippoorwill,

no arguments heard from cow birds,

killdeers or blue jays, only silence,
for even the crows have up and moved
to the city.

Country Feed Supply

As Winter tries to close its fist
on the furrowed fields
where discs turn
for the umpteenth time, there's a memory
in the kernels of corn
dormant 'til Spring— a memory of green,
a memory of gold, a memory of shoots
and roots to behold.

It's a miracle of darkness
and the blessing of light
when sun warms seeds to life.
The unfurling of Spring
is the beauty of God, peace
to Summer, praise
to storm, food on the table
and the chattel floor.

From field to hopper,
from hopper to bin, from bin to truck
then up and up
the Country Feed Store's sixty-five foot

grain-leg* drop. Feed for horses,
feed for pigs, feed for cattle,
chicken and eggs. One bag, two,
three bags full
of the sweetest seeds— non-GMO.

*grain-leg— sheet metal round vent that the grain
travels through to get bagged.

Country Feed Supply on Kittle Road

If I were nature I'd have plenty of good things to say about Country Feed Supply in Mio. For starters, much of the feed out the door is non-GMO. That means it is real food for real farm animals and pets. If I were a horse, I'd be shaking my head up and down with a happy whinny about the organic alternatives to Roundup-Ready Corn and beans. I'd smile if I were a lamb, a pig or a dog in need of good feed.

A very high percentage of The Country Feed Store seed for crops is also non-GMO. This is quite a challenge given that widespread cross pollination from GMO fields has tainted our organic seed bank at an alarming rate. I highly commend the Feed Store partners for taking the time and effort to accommodate those of us that do not believe in Monsanto's meddling with God given genes. As a disclaimer, the above views are my own and are not necessarily the views of The Country Feed Store.

Just ask the caring and knowledgeable staff in the store for help finding the right alternatives to GMO products if you are of a like mind as myself. They do as well stock and sell Monsanto's breed of seed and feed.

The Country Feed Store also caters to recreational bird feeding. They carry a vast store of products from feeders to seeds for your bird watching enjoyment. The Amish Country's habitat for bird species is very large and diverse. We have cardinals, finches, woodpeckers, warblers, jays and many, many other species in our winter feeders. As a proactive measure, bird feeders taken in at night helps curb feeder and property damage from roaming black bears during spring and summer months.

Speaking of game, the store also carries everything you need for deer and turkey food plots. They carry all your fencing and animal control needs. I even found out they carry a natural pesticide for those pesky potato bugs called Spinosad which is derived from the fermentation of a specific bacteria. Last but not least they carry organic based weed control products called tines, rakes and hoes.

Dance in the Dark

It is on occasion, after a day of drenching rain,
they come out to play. Rain is music to their earthly
souls, a primitive reminder of the percussion of sex,
the need to partner-up and get down to some
serious love making in the wet grass and dirt as
lightning bugs and stars ramp up to flicker.

In the Amish Country, night crawlers are not
neighborhood hoodlums with their underwear and
butt cracks showing. They don't hang around on
street corners at two o'clock in the morning smoking
pot. They aren't out dealing Meth or accosting
senior citizens for some meager amount of cash to
buy a hit of crack cocaine.

In this neck of the woods, night crawlers are quiet
and helpful. They are industrious. They spend
their days and most nights out of view burrowing
about and enhancing the richness of our everyday
lives for the pure joy of it. Their underground

farming endeavors, unbeknownst to most, help feed the world; and for all you democratic socialists out there, you don't even get charged for their vast experience in soil work, they do it for free.

I confess that I remain unamused by the human cults of socialism. I want to be free to create and get paid a fair price for what I do. Writing is a time consuming occupation and words as well as the paper they are printed on have no nutritional value unto themselves. Their value lies in the realm of spiritual and emotional food for readers willing to trade a piece of their income produced from occupations such as sawing wood or planting crops, building boats or mowing lawns. To put it bluntly, just as the night crawler cannot survive without soil and water, I cannot survive without readers buying my books. So please, please do.

Night crawlers gloriously present themselves in the night after a nice soaking rain by emerging from the earth and stretching out on the surface to bask naked in the starlight. They often find a willing partner and commingle in their night crawler secretions. They test their powers of elasticity and speed by keeping their butt ends in the earth and retracting quickly if you should disturb their bliss with heavy feet or a bright flashlight. When entering to trod there, you must be quiet and respectful of their world.

A dim flashlight swung slowly in an arc discerns their glistening presence on the periphery of the beam. It's in this half-light one must snatch them with quick hands and a gentle touch to extract their tail end without breaking them in half. Picking crawlers is an art, it is a dance in the dark. It is a communion in the chain of life that keeps man humble and in touch with his place in the grand scheme of all living things. We, as humans, are not Gods, we are caretakers intimately tied to nature's cycles of give and take. We sow and we reap. We balance the scales or pay the price.

5:00 AM

A hint that the day
has begun
are the dove's
coo from the dawn's
dark magic
where eyes seek
things not there.

A black bear
approaches invisible
so why pretend.
The deer
are ghosts of old
tree stumps left
to remind us
that our mortal days
come numbered.

Among the gatherings
of wrens and warblers
about the yard, some argue

as others taunt, but most
rejoice in singing
as the sky cracks pearly blue
as a robin's egg.

The Stallion

What remains
of the apples
is cider
and the deer.
The north
is storming south
with a wolfish grin
wheedled by the wind
and fury is born
in the wild-
eyed horse
flinging its mane
and rearing before it—
hell shrieks and steam
wheezing
from the beast
like smoke
and harried the geese
and widgeon hiss
and grappling limbs
of aspen crack
like whips on the Michigan shore.

USA Handcrafted Solid Wood Furniture

When it comes to USA made, Oak Hill Furniture and Fabrics of Mio lives up to that distinction. Not only is their furniture USA grown and produced, it is superbly handcrafted and very reasonably priced.

If you are a parent or grandparent looking for that special cradle, crib bed, rocking horse or chair, Oak Hill is a must stop while you are in the Amish Country. Their convertible cribs transform to fit the growth and needs of your youngster throughout childhood and beyond. Each handcrafted piece is skillfully crafted of solid woods individually selected for their color and grain.

They have a generous selection of in store furnishings to browse, yet all items can be custom ordered and built from over 50 different wood and color combinations including oak, cherry, maple, walnut, hickory and birch. Once your custom order is placed, your wish list pieces are handcrafted by deft hands from Millersburg, Walnut Creek or

Fredericksburg, Ohio and delivered in 8 to 12 weeks. There is no added cost for getting your furnishings customized to enhance and fit your own personal decor.

If you are in the market for a mattress, Oak Hill carries an assortment of USA Country Bedding mattresses with ten year warranties. You'll also discover a large selection of wood case clocks and decorative pieces for wall and mantle. As a bonus, they have a variety of fabrics, yarns and supplies for those creative quilt and home sewing projects, including USA Denim tri-blend.

Oak Hill Furniture and Fabrics is owned and operated by Melvin and Betty Byler. It is located in the lovely Amish countryside on Gailbraith Road just north of highway F32 (Miller Road). Very highly recommended.

Snow Birds

The hardwoods
have turned
magical
with their robes of gold,
red and orange.
The apples glow.

The pumpkins
smile
and flicker like ghouls
as the children settle
into desks at school.

Wood smoke whirls
with scented wisps
of smoked fish and brisket
barbecue. The sky
is full of geese and teal
skedaddling south
with a dirge I've heard
for sixty years.

Capturing the Amish Country Music Scene

The Amish Country has its share of good Music. You can capture its resonance with your ears, your heart or in the case of Judy and Lisa— through the eye and lens of a Nikon or Canon.

Northern Exposure Photography and Arts has become a name synonymous with the Northeastern Michigan music scene ever since Lisa and Judy started shooting Friday Night Fireside Music Events at the Skyline Event Center in Comins. It was there that Northern Exposure found their passion and knack for adeptly capturing the band members and musicians within the framework of live photography. Now, tens of thousands of shots later, this photo-happy duo find themselves fast becoming the official photographers for such mainline events as the Nor-East'r Music and Arts Festival. You will also find them snapping away at Riverfest and the Thunder Bay Folk Festival.

Northern Exposure Photography and Arts has been able to capture those perfect moments for use in media publications, for enhancing band promotions as well as artistic presentations. Judy and Lisa are also available for hire to professionally shoot small weddings, graduations, sporting and group events as well as family and pet portraits.

Northern Exposure's online gallery can be found at: nephotoandarts.zenfolio.com.

If you would like to visit Lisa and Judy's physical gallery which includes photos, pottery and other crafts, their contact information is: nephotoandarts@gmail.com

Curmudgeon

There's a depth
to his eyes
where the night skies
twinkle.

There's a beat
in his heart
where the old man
dances.

Deception

In a stubbled field
of corn dusted
with frost, a majestic
and regal
bald eagle
rips the intestines
from a mouse.

The Henhouse

The bickering has begun
among the disturbed
chickens in the henhouse.

A rooster flew in
from New York
and crowed unexpectedly.

The chickens are scared.
They fear for their eggs
and entitlements.

He's just too cocky
with his combover crown
and rebellious nature.

The hens cackle
and berate him, they squawk
and bawk* their wattle.

The rooster laughs
and struts even prouder
he's got their feathers up.

*bawk- the sound chickens make.

Shady Lane Footwear

Shady Lane Footwear is an Amish Country shoe store without Saks Fifth Avenue foot traffic. No one goes out for a walk, notices a flashy sign and decides it's time to go shoe shopping at Shady Lane Footwear. You get there by word of mouth, a good sense of direction or a car with g.p.s. navigation. The shoe shop is on Bills Road off Kittle Road beyond the Country Corners Bulk Food Store in a far-out location in the Mio countryside.

They don't stock city shoes like high heels or blue suede at Shady Lane, but they do have muck boots and steel toed clod hoppers. They have a wide assortment of top brand footwear for kids, women and men in regular and unusual sizes. Their enormous selection of high quality shoes and boots includes over thirty different top brand names such as Ariat, Wolverine, Red Wing, Sketchers, Bogs, etc. Eleven of those brands are made not in China or Vietnam, but right here in the good old US of A.

Shady Lane also carries a variety of socks, belts and gloves for all the different Michigan weather extremes.

For the frugal shopper and bargain hunter, their clearance shelf is generously arrayed with display-model or discontinued items. Shady Lane is one of those old country places of which your weary feet have dreams. It is a boot and shoe oasis.

Calvin and his family not only take care of your feet, but come summer they are Amish Country suppliers of home grown vegetables, fruits and berries at the Lone Pine farmers market near the corner of Kittle Road and M33. You'll find their strawberries and vegetables sprinkled with morning dew instead of Monsanto chemicals. As for the taste, pure Sunshine!

So don't be shy, stop by, say hi and may your feet grow wings.

Magpies

Where bare branch
fingers sky
they congregate, gossips in tree tops
cackling birdbrained
as the moon sets
quarter drained.

Down at the church
autumn has come
frozen toed
in winter shoes.
It's the first Tuesday
of November
as voters slip
into a booth to confess,
not to a priest or God,
but the Devil's rule
for the next four years.

The magpies
shuffle uncomfortable on their perch, turn
their yellow eyes toward heaven
and explode into a storm.

Jalapeño Bowels

Today was a disturbance
of the peace. It was broken.
Protesters congregated.
Anarchists raised their fists.
The police showed up
with riot gear and teargas.
Some days are like this.
So much unrest within the boundaries
of our lives. I want to scream
at the nonsense. There is too much
shoving and foul language. It is rude.
Just miserable as the weather.
Irritable as jalapeño bowels.

Ice Fishing While Watching the News

I sit here
on the ice
jigging a minnow.
I want to feel
empathy for
its eventual demise
to a bigger fish, but
I realize
the irony and foolishness of that
kind of thinking. All fish
are cannibalistic.
Their behavior is like our nation's
ill-mannered leftists
and media ever since
we the "deplorables"
elected Donald Trump.

If a newscaster knew
how to catch a fish
instead of being the fish, I might show
some semblance of respect.

I might even catch
and release, honor them for
the pure sport of it, maybe even
pardon their ignorance
and fish school mentality; but since
the election
all I have heard
is their bitter gnash
of carnivorous teeth. They are like
frenzied piranhas.

I had an inkling that such evil
possibly existed, but
I had no idea
of the covert wrath
lying just beneath the placid
social surface. The leftist
facade of decency
revealed itself to be
deceptive as the smile
of Hillary Clinton. I now have
no qualms about letting
these shallow fish swallow
the proverbial hook, gasp for breath and fry
in a pan of hot oil.

The liberals are the ones
that took the bait in the first place. When Saul
Alinsky* jigged his radical jig,
they bit. When Bill Ayers*
and the Students for a Democratic Society* trolled
the campuses, they bit. When Timothy Leary*
chummed
a lost generation with mescaline
and LSD, they bit. When Bill Clinton
made adulterous blow jobs in the White House
fit for a president, they bit. When academia tossed
the addled brain of Bernie Sanders
into the mix, they bit. So
if you are crazy enough to bite
and believe in that shit
you more than deserve Donald Trump.

*Saul Alinsky- self-proclaimed communist that wrote
the book Rules for Radicals embraced as the
Political Bible by Hillary Clinton and Barrack
Obama.
*Bill Ayers- domestic terrorist and murderer free on
legal technicalities.

*Timothy Leary- perpetrator of synthetic LSD.
A CIA operative that infiltrated the 60's youth
movement to destroy it's effectiveness with drugs.
*Students for a Democratic Society- domestic
terrorist organization.

Jigs-Up

Fishing has been an integral part of life even before Jesus turned water into wine. But unlike Jesus, us mortals need more than just a word— we need rods, reels, and bait to fish. We need a net, monofilament, hooks, lures and a boat full of luck. The place to get these things in the Amish Country is at Jigs-Up Bait and Tackle on Mt. Tom Road north of the river. The catchy and colorful bait shop name came about when William (Hooch) Hoover netted a huge rainbow trout and called out to others in the boat, "Jigs up". For me, the name conjures up leprechauns, mermaids and whale-tales of a fish story or two.

Dave Welters, the bait shop owner, once fell through the ice on a day when Mio Pond temperatures had plummeted to twenty-one below zero. He lived and still stands behind the counter at Jigs-Up to tell you about it. That's some pretty decent luck in my book and luck is what most fishermen want to hear about when they stop by the local bait-shop. Besides purchasing bait and tackle, they want to know the latest hot spot, technique and baits being used to land those big ones. They want to see photos of mythical lunkers pinned to the bait shop bulletin board. They want to stretch the truth to the point of snapping the line regarding the ones that got away.

Besides the bait, Dave loves to tinker and repair those old boat motors that were born before the 1980's. He speaks reverently of those dinosaur Evinrudes, Johnsons and Scott-Atwaters that had a simple yet mechanical genius to their works. So, please don't toss or bury those relics in a landfill, take them to Dave at Jigs-Up for one last look and a shot at hooking one more big one on the AuSable.

The Blue Spruce

The blue spruce paints Christmas in the heart
of the evergreen forest as families depart
their jobs to join Heaven's light and share
candied ham, buttered peas and loving care.

The blushed blue needles winter glow
soft and iridescent with powdered snow,
her perfume robust as bitters of gin
when icicles hang from eaves and chin.

We wade thigh high through drifts in search
of the perfect top and perfect perch
for four calling birds and three French hens,
two turtle doves on a Christmas limb

and a partridge in a blue spruce tree.

Forty Below

The sun
lacking warmth is piercing
needles of light.
My eyes burn, water and blur
blind and shut. They seek
the darkness and comfort
of earth beneath snow
as white and deep as January.

This is how it feels
to be buried alive like a blade of grass,
smothered and choked like asparagus
too long in the freezer. These are the shivers
of a naked rose
at forty below gone nuclear.

The wind is more
guilty than innocent when it blows into town
strung out on frostbite. The ears have to bear
their own vivid screams, and the toes go deaf
and dumb as the feet that stumble
to get over themselves.

You cannot fathom the frigid squirrel
of black tires
on a worried bicycle. Michigan
shouldn't be this miserable. Our home
shouldn't be so cold.

Christmas Day

In Glennie Creek's
teepee hummocks—
the mice are busy
wrapping nuts
and cherries dried
in tufts of summer.

The fresh snow
flutters and winks
diamond chinks
in the sunlight.
Among wind torn
thorn-berry trees
chickadees perch
ruffled against
the relentless cold.

In the hearth fire—
hickory logs
snap, snap
like smacking lips
savoring Christmas

chocolates
and eggnogs spiked
with sweet brandy
and peppermint schnapps.

The turkey comes
wafting hot
out of the oven
with baked beans
and cranberry muffins,
crusted bread
and sage stuffing
blessed and buttery
as my sweetheart's kiss.

QuickTurtle Books® author
Mary Rensberry

Mary Rensberry's endearing accent and angelic spirit recently captivated a live audience at the Skyline Event Center in Comins, during a reading of her book Christmas Christmas Everyday. Her bright smile and generous heart revealed themselves to be as broad and expansive as the great State of Texas in which she was born and raised.

As a recent transplant to Fairview, Michigan from California, Mary has brought with her not only her uplifting perspective but also QuickTurtle Books®.

In combination with the Rensberry's move to the Amish Country and her long and distinguished teaching career in which she taught children of all ages, Mary's life long inspiration to write and publish has found fertile ground in which to grow. "Children," she reveled, "are endowed with a vast reservoir of curiosity and joy. They are spontaneous and receptive to help and helping, willing to be self-determined while simultaneously empathizing with others. I believe all of us are capable of maintaining and nurturing such virtues."

In her recent book-- I AM SPIRIT-- that is exactly what Mary Rensberry set out to accomplish. In collaboration with award winning Amsterdam artist Junai Meijer, Mary has created, in simple yet dynamic terms— the ABC's of an Ideal Spirit. This hardback book is beautifully conceptualized and emotes a strong wavelength that coincides with man's higher self. It is comprised of the essence, power and virtues of positive thinking, making the book's message both spiritual and irresistible.

"We knowingly or unknowingly create the world around us in an image of ourselves," Mary explained. "Reality is the manifestation of our thoughts. As spirits, we have a choice as to which reality we wish to nurture and live in."

Mary currently is in the process of converting and producing I AM SPIRIT into a helpful and powerful flipbook for use in home, office and school. Each page erupts with bright colors and an equally bright message that is sure to uplift and inspire its readers each and every day of the year.

You can find Mary's books in The Family Bookshelf in Fairview and other local bookstores. They are also available online at Ingram Spark and Amazon.com. I Am Spirit can also be ordered directly from Mary at:
maryandrichard@quickturtlebooks.com

Dreamer of Dreams

I'm a dreamer
of dreams with eyes
wide open. I see
what is
and what isn't
seen, imagined or magical
when it comes to hands
waved
and fingers snapped
in an act of theft
of what is left
of God.

I'm a dreamer of dreams
in stereo
surround sound.
I hear
the angels speak
as demons sneak
beneath our joys. I hear
the noise in silence
and the silence in noise.

I'm a dreamer
of dreams
on fertile earth
with seeds strewn
into the future of worth
where seasons turn
from lies
to truth, and men
grow bigger
than the ego of sin.

Your Own Bare Hands

Have you ever
seen a farmer reap wheat with a team
of yoked horses? Children
dance ecstatically across an open
field? Ten year old boys
in command of machines
that would scare the bejeezus
out of full grown men?
Have you ever?

Seen a fire blue-hot
forge iron in a blacksmith's shop? Have you?
hit a chisel with a sledge? Seen
a mill stone turn
to grind flour for bread? Have you ever
milked a cow or bled
a chicken with your own bare hands?

Have you ever
had to drink from a puddle of mud
or turn a cow into leather
boots? Had to?

walk for miles to find your humble way
out of the deep, deep woods? Have you ever
had to sleep on a rock for warmth
or run in the pitch black dark?

Have you ever thought
that the world around us
was a runaway bus?
in need of your hands on the wheel?

Afterword

When I undertook the writing of "City Slicker's Guide to the Amish Country" I had no idea of the perseverance I was going to need to take it to completion. The amount of patience and time involved with meeting and establishing communication with the contributors within the margins of this book was an experience I value more than the book itself. I have a deep respect for the pioneer spirit of men and women willing to forge a living from the fruitful lands of their heart and ingenuity. I hope you the reader can garner from within these pages the hard work and fortitude needed to establish and maintain a true and prospering community in rural America. The fruits of these individuals with the strength and moral fiber to endure— are happiness, pride and prosperity, not only for themselves but for their families, friends and those they knowingly and unknowingly touch. May God bless the men and women of the Amish Country for their contribution to this book and the State of Michigan.

Reader support of local businesses and attractions in rural America goes far in providing the where-with-all for its residents to prosper and create jobs for their families and local youth. Please take the time to browse and frequent the businesses and attractions described within the contents of this book as well as those listed in the business section that immediately follows.

Thank You, Richard Rensberry

Please Support Local Businesses:

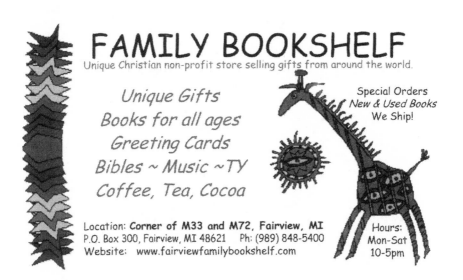

Richard & Mary Rensberry

uickTurtle Books®

510-579-2290   **510-688-1849**

Amish Country Natural Products

989-390-5915

Natural/Organic Foods
Artisan Breads
Michigan Made Gifts

Roxanne Striggow
Owner

1454 N. Mt Tom Road	Like Us On Facebook
Mio, Mi 48647	amishcountrynaturalprdcts@gmail.com

Oscoda County Art Council

www.timberlandquilttrail.org

P.O. Box 777 Mio, Michigan 48647

Contact: Susan Shantz, Coordinator

989-848-5757

Melodic Sounds Studio

Piano Lessons

with Jade Parker-Kozlow

989-390-4001

Facebook: melodic sounds studio

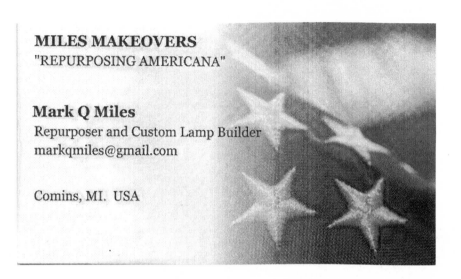

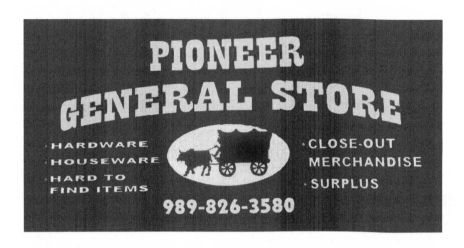

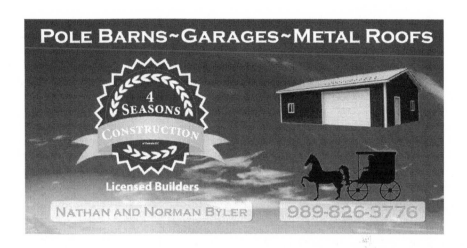

Sunrise Thrift Shop
989-390-0180

Located in
Bo-Ton Plaza
Fairview, MI

Steiner Museum

www.thesteinermuseum.org

989-889-1742

Highway M-33 at 1980 Reber Road

Made in the USA
Lexington, KY
14 April 2017